MY MOTHER'S STORY

My Mother's Story

by
Sonia Alland

Pinyon Publishing
Montrose, CO

Cover and Interior Art Copyright by Sonia Alland

Thanks to Denis Medvedsek for scanning the original photographs appearing on the cover and page ix:

Cover: *My Mother at Possibly 19 Years of Age*

Page ix: *My Mother and Me in California*

Back Cover Photograph of Sonia Alland by Denis Medvedsek

First Edition: February 2021

Pinyon Publishing
23847 V66 Trail, Montrose, CO 81403
www.pinyon-publishing.com

Library of Congress Control Number: 2021931039
ISBN: 978-1-936671-73-1

With this text, I would like to honor the memory of my mother with the esteem and respect she richly deserved and preserve the image of the woman who has emerged from the retelling.

Contents

Preface

MY mother, Rose Feldman, née Rose Cohn, was born in Minsk, Belorussia, on or around November 9, 1895. She was unsure of the exact date. She died on August 31st, 1992, close to 97 years of age, the day I arrived back in New York City from France. She knew the date I would be back in New York and held out until that day, but died before I could make it to Florida to be at her side. In one of our conversations during her last years, I had promised her I'd be sure she was dead before she was cremated. (It's not the custom for Jewish people to cremate the dead but my mother, not a devout Jew, preferred being cremated over the disagreeable idea of being covered with dirt.) In any event, I phoned the officiating doctor to confirm that she had really died. One can imagine my embarrassment; nevertheless, though I failed to be with her when she died, I was determined to at least fulfill my promise. The doctor confirmed that there was no mistake. She had, indeed, passed away.

We were four offspring in the family: three girls and one boy. I was the youngest and, of the girls, I think the closest to my mother. Over the years, I was the observer of her unhappy marriage and also an unhappy participant in it. I was painfully aware of her distress and sometime during adolescence grew to feel that I should be her moral support, which is what, as a young adult, I believe I became.

Some years ago, as a young mother, I wrote a short narrative about my mother, who was, then, still alive and, though we resided at opposite sides of the continent, very much present, at least in my thoughts. Writing the piece put me into another world, a welcome change from the demands of domestic life: raising two children and dealing with the tensions one so often experiences in the early years of married life. I also wrote a story about my brother that flowed out seamlessly, as if already written inside me. I'm sure, in some way, I identified with this brother and yearned to tell his story. I've decided to add it as an addendum to the memoir of our mother. His life and his relationship to our father are intricately related to our mother's story.

In the last few years, along with other interests, I've turned to translation, from the French, in which I've been fluent for some time, and Catalan, a more recent acquisition. Recently, I've been immersed in the translation of a memoir by a Catalan writer, Maria Mercè Roca. When my old and dear friends, Stuart Friebert* and Diane Vreuls, both writers and, Stuart, a translator as well, read the manuscript of Roca's memoir and "My Brother's Story," both insisted that, instead of solely translating the works of others, I should turn to composing my own texts. Their encouragement, and my recent immersion in the Roca memoir, inspired me to take another look at the memoir I'd begun years ago of my mother and to rework it into what would be a more elaborate text on my mother's life, one which, inevitably, would have references to my own life. Without my friends' encouragement, the narrative that follows would never have been written. I am deeply grateful to them for their friendship and their support.

---

* Stuart is no longer with us. He died on June 23, 2020.

My Mother's Story

AROUND 120 years ago in the hold of an ocean liner heading for the promised land, the United States of America, a little four-year-old, who would grow up to be my mother, was squeezed among bundles of food and belongings with her own mother and father and two of her sisters and five brothers. The voyage was long and miserable. (My mother at more than 96 years of age still remembered the smells.) But like all children, she probably found others to play with and do what children do with the energy of young life. It was the harassed mother, nauseous as she must have been in the airless stink of that closed in space, who had to care for her brood of children, with, hopefully, some help from her husband who, being a teacher and, as we'll see, eager to learn himself, may have found a book that occupied him much of the time, distracting him from the unpleasantness surrounding them.

Upon arriving in the United States, the family went to Cleveland, Ohio, where the family had distant relatives who had made the ocean crossing some years before and where my mother's eldest sister — the most enterprising of the girls — was lodging. I remember being told she'd stayed for a while with these relatives, but had she traveled by herself to the States before the rest of the family? That seems unreal: a young girl perhaps 16 or 17 traveling on her own. Perhaps she accompanied these relatives on the voyage, but I can't be sure. I do know that she was living with them for a time and, becoming pregnant in a relationship with the young man of the household, had to marry him. But more of that later.

My mother's parents rented a house much too small for the large family, but with little means, they had no choice. Her father was a private teacher and, in those days, teachers, let alone tutors, earned very little money. Though he had been highly respected in his own city, Minsk, and many parents sent their boys to him to prepare them to compete for the few places allotted Jewish youths in the gymnasium—the high school—in his new home he was unknown and would have to build up his reputation again as a private tutor. And what could he teach? My mother in her affectionate recollections of her father spoke of him as a teacher but never specified what he taught. Perhaps there was a rare student interested in learning Russian, though not the numbers he may have helped to pass the gymnasium exam in Minsk. More likely, he found some youngsters who needed tutoring in Hebrew for their Bar Mitzvah or, though my grandfather was not religious, he may have had sufficient studies of the Talmud to also tutor it to young Jewish scholars. I can be certain, however, that the one subject he did not teach was English as he himself had no knowledge of it. As the head of the family in this unfamiliar world, he needed to speak English and, indeed, he had a great desire to speak it, so much so that he apparently asked permission to attend children's classes. It seems they were third graders. And, determined, not minding the embarrassment of being an adult among children, he achieved a fine level of English. There is a letter to his son, in English, that my mother, perhaps because of her attachment to her father, had found and put away and that I, in turn, found, after her death, and kept. It's clearly written and in careful, neat penmanship, that attests to his having been a diligent student of the language: a sad letter—a document that concerns a past distressful event. More about that later, as well.

Whatever my mother's father earned from what was probably just a few hours of lessons, perhaps not even every day, was not enough to take care of the family. The children needed food, clothing. Rent had to be paid. Her mother wanted to make wholesome meals but for so many children — and she'd given birth to one more little boy — she often had nothing but watery soup to serve all of them. (Though my mother remembers her father bringing home a little meat every Friday for the Sabbath meal and everyone had a bite-size portion.) And she couldn't help but complain. Why does he read so much, always with "his nose in a book," she would say. But she knew her husband could not change and, we can only conjecture, she may have respected his need to read and learn. In any event, she had to look elsewhere for a solution to her problems.

Crowded as the house was, the mother finally decided to take in boarders. It meant more work for her, but the extra income kept them alive. There were days when she did not feel well, but burdened with tasks, there was not a minute in the day when she could rest.

The years went by and the children were growing up. Three of the four sisters were considered old enough to go to work, though the youngest of the three, Ida, was just fourteen. Meager as the factory salaries were, they helped support the family. Fanny, the eldest, was a good student, however. In those days, many young people did not complete their high school education, but Fanny was determined to have her high school diploma. Her father, of course, encouraged her desire for an education, though this meant that Fanny couldn't contribute to the household like the other two. Her education would have priority. Fanny is the daughter who lived for a while with the distant relatives. This perplexes me. Did she live with the relatives while going to high school? Is that when she had a relationship with the young man of the household and became pregnant? I do remember my mother saying that her mother would tell Fanny to cover herself with a shawl while going to the outhouse at the end of the yard so that the neighbors wouldn't see her swollen figure. Why would her mother be embarrassed if her daughter were already married to the distant cousin? Or perhaps she wasn't married yet and only when she could no longer hide her pregnancy did she consent to marry the fellow. At times I feel like a detective reconstituting a logical sequence of events, making sense from memories of events related to me over many years, or from my own observations as I was growing up. And there are frustrating lacunae. I do know that this sister, my Aunt Fanny, was ambitious: she became a registered nurse, a huge accomplishment at the time and, especially, for one from an impoverished family. I also know that she had not one but two children with her distant cousin and found herself in an unhappy marriage. In fact, when her children were little, she left her husband for another man, and abandoned them. They never forgave her, feelings no doubt fomented by her rejected husband's anger. I can share an anecdote with you that illustrates their deep resentment. Aunt Fanny, already a nurse, learned that one of her sons was very ill. She managed to get to his bedside but he literally turned his back on her. When my mother described the scene, I felt I was there. I could see the child (in my imagination, as I'd never met him) rejecting his mother and her grief at not being able to care for her sick son. But these vivid mental scenes—I can hardly call them memories—don't help me establish the sequence of events: when did Fanny get pregnant? If not as a high school student, was it when she was studying to be a nurse? Was she already a nurse when she left her children and married her beloved second husband? We'll never know. Though it would be satisfying to know the sequence of events, perhaps it's not important. We already have an idea of what Aunt Fanny was like. We'll see some more of this sister in our story.

My mother told me very little about her sisters as adolescents. I can imagine Fanny studying for her courses in high school—and working perhaps at odd jobs after school—while the two younger sisters, Esther and Ida, worked long days in a small clothing factory. Most of their meager salaries, if not all, went to their mother, though it was hardly enough to pay for the clothes they and their little brothers required. With such active little boys even knee patches didn't last. Many a Sunday—a scene my mother did indeed describe to me—Ida or Esther would spend their only day off sitting at the family sewing machine quickly putting together the stack of pieces that their mother had cut out in the proper size for the pants that each of the six growing boys needed.

And now a word about Rose, the youngest of the four girls, who would, one day, be my mother. She was only eleven at this point in our narrative, too young for factory work and still in school, though her schooling was to end before she completed the sixth grade. Her mother who never stopped cleaning and cooking and sewing, even when she didn't feel well, grew progressively sicker. Rose, after school, would help with the cleaning and cooking that still had to be done. The doctor didn't know exactly what was bothering her mother. He thought it was her stomach and gave her medicine for stomach trouble. (Remember, this is medical care by a local doctor during the early 1900s.) But, as the months went on, Rose's mother grew weaker. Finally, the doctor realized what was wrong. Rose's mother had tuberculosis, and probably had had it for a long time. At that point, however, it was a very bad case and, in any event, there was no cure for the disease.

Fresh air was said to help. As a last resort, Rose was taken out of school and sent with her mother and the little brothers to a house that their father rented for them in the country. He had to work in the city where he continued to live with his older daughters, but he came to visit on the weekends.

Rose's mother could barely get out of bed. It was up to the eleven-year-old to take care of her two little brothers. There was no running water in the house. Rose filled up pails from the pump in the yard. She also carted in the coal for their furnace. When my mother described the situation, she never shared any feelings of resentment about working so hard. Perhaps she felt proud assuming the tasks of a "big person," ones that her mother would normally do. However, caring for a mother in the last stages of tuberculosis and looking after young brothers was surely an undue burden for the child. In coping with this early experience, I'm wondering if it in some way prepared her for what was to come later in life.

After a few months, Rose's father could see his wife was not getting better from the country air. In fact, she seemed to be more weak and sick every time he came to visit. At last, he moved Rose, her mother and the brothers back to their home in the city. They would all be together that way for his wife's remaining days.

She died soon after her return home. Though not the best provider, he had loved his wife deeply and missed her, but he knew his children were in need of the care only a mother could give. He thought of his wife's sister who had always wanted to marry him. She was a good deal older than he was, not the attractive woman his wife had been, and not so pleasant a person as her sister, but the father was sure that, because she was already an aunt to the children, she would find it natural to take care of them and love them as her own.

How wrong he was! Unfortunately, he did not discover his mistake until after his marriage. The children's aunt was more than unpleasant. She had a nasty temper and beat the little boys if they disturbed her with their noise. He had to put an end to this violence and as a temporary solution, put the two youngest boys, Louie and Albert, in an orphanage where they could be kept out of trouble for a time. Unbeknownst to anyone, Albert was suffering the effects of tuberculosis, contracted, it seems, from his ailing mother when she gave birth to him or soon after. It apparently did not affect his lungs as tuberculosis commonly does but, rather, his testicles, which had to be removed, I believe I was told — I'm not sure of certain "memories" — at age thirteen. Either he had already passed puberty at that age or, as his father's letter to him suggests, he had the operation, not at thirteen, but as a young adult. When I knew him, he was probably in his forties and had the attributes of a normal male. He also may have had hormone treatments, possible in the 1940s. Be that as it may, I have fond memories of my dear Uncle Albert. He would have been a loving father but never married or had children of his own. However, for his nieces, he was a kind, gentle person who always had some little treat when he came to visit, cheering us up with his calm, sunny manner.

But we're jumping ahead. Let us return to my mother, Rose, and her childhood. We know that there was very little money and, as always, it was a difficult job to feed everyone. The children were neglected and hungry. Fanny, from her after-school jobs, as well as Ida and Esther, managed to spend some of the money they earned on extra food, which they ate while out of the house. But Rose, instead of returning to school, had stayed at home to help her aunt. She could only eat what she found in the house. Luckily there was a restaurant nearby with huge garbage cans near the back exit. Rose often peeked into the cans as she passed to do some errands for her aunt. Most of the time she would find fresh-pressed oranges thrown out after the juice was extracted every morning in preparation for the breakfast menu. She remembered the taste and the fragrant odor of the fruit's juicy pulp for the rest of her life. In her nineties, she told her grandchild, Julie—

my daughter, an artist—about the oranges and today I can see the results in a piece dedicated to her Grandma Rose: slices of oranges integrated into a bas-relief she created in honor of her grandmother.

So much to tell about my mother's long life, it's easy to lose the thread. Let's pick it up again with her father. Though his teaching took him out of the house, before long it was obvious to him that his wife's sister was not a good mother for his children. Why else, in heaven's name, had he married her? Clearly, staying married to this harsh woman would not provide his children with the motherly affection they needed, so, as quickly as possible, he found a way of divorcing this second wife. Yet, divorces, in the early years of the 20th century, were not common and, most likely, not easy to obtain. How did my grandfather do it? What arguments did he use? Did he have to pay a lawyer's fees? If so, where did the money come from? Questions for which I have only conjecture, no answers. Though uncomfortable at not having all the answers, let us console ourselves with the knowledge that he did, indeed, get his divorce. And proceed with our story.

For several years Rose, a young teenager, took care of the family as best she could. Meanwhile, Fanny had gone on with her studies and would eventually complete her nurse's training. We know she married the distant cousin, the father of her two boys, and lived in a comfortable house. We also know that she was not happy in her marriage and would soon leave her husband and her two children but, in the meantime, she lived well. She was a good cook and, at least once a week, baked delicious cookies and cakes. Rose came to visit and would smell the fresh-baked pastries. When was the last time she'd eaten a pastry? She couldn't even remember. She longed for a taste but didn't feel right asking her older sister for one. And Fanny, though she knew full well how poorly Rose and the others ate at home, never offered her young sister even a small bite of a sweet. Fanny was clever and lively company and Rose continued to visit, yet, on leaving Fanny's house, how could she not help feeling bewildered and hurt by her sister's ungenerous nature. And Fanny continued to act with selfish self-interest, not simply by depriving her younger sister of something good to eat but by causing hardship. Many years later, when my mother was bound in an unhappy marriage, Fanny filled my father's ears with negative comments about his wife, and in so doing, by comparing what she would have done, enhancing her own image. Later, my father would accuse my mother of her faults, citing her sister Fanny. I wonder if my mother ever forgave her. I find it hard to.

Rose continued to keep house while Esther and Ida worked to help support the family. The four older brothers were probably, by this time, pursuing their education. Harold, I knew, would become a physician; Maurice, a pharmacist; Bob would volunteer in World War I, and Jack, the eldest, eventually settled in Canada. Louie and Albert—sick but no one realized to what extent until much later—had been reintegrated into the family. She tried to be a good housekeeper and take care of the boys, but her father, a kind man, knew it was too difficult for one so young. He too was growing weary of living without a wife. He needed a woman's companionship. One day, he announced to Esther, Ida, and Rose that he was going to marry once more. This time the woman was perfect! Not only beautiful, but generous and intelligent. In short, he loved her and knew she would be the ideal wife and mother.

However when the daughters met their future stepmother, they saw her with different eyes. She was much younger than their father—just a few years older than Fanny. It was obvious to them that their father was blind to her true feelings. They could sense that she would take what she could from their kind but foolish father and then leave him. They warned him. They pleaded with him. But their father was decided. He married his young lady. Soon after he borrowed enough money to buy his new wife a small diamond ring, she left him. Sadly enough, his daughters' predictions were fulfilled.

Years later, after yet another poor choice for a wife — my grandfather apparently could not do without female companionship, his daughters aside — he married a sweet little lady who was kind and loving to him during his last years. By my count, this was his fifth wife! At last, before it was too late, he found the happiness in marriage he had, I imagine, with his first wife, the mother of his children, at least during their early years, when she was a beautiful, and healthy, young woman.

But let us return to my mother and her three sisters. We know that Fanny was unhappily married and no longer lived at home. Esther married as well. Her husband worked hard and developed a thriving construction business. Even before their two sons were old enough to help their father in his business, Esther and her husband were able to buy a house and live very well. Esther, that is, could have lived well, but she was forged by her childhood: the thin soup her mother used to make, the long, tiring hours in the factory and the pitifully small salary she received at the end of each week. She had learned to save penny by penny to help the rest of the family and still be able to buy a pair of shoes she desperately needed. So accustomed had she become to saving that though her husband now earned a comfortable living, she could not change her habits, nor could she rid herself of the feeling of being deprived. Though my mother, ever a caring sister, would spend hours on the phone listening to the constant complaints my "sad-sack" aunt poured into her ear, she complained to me that her sister, rather than spend money on a dress, would wear her old, worn clothes and would save money in countless other ways, like buying the cheapest cuts of meat. In her mind, she was still in her father's house. I'm sure that she, like my mother, would have a story to tell if someone, other than my mother who is long gone, were still around to tell it.

Ida, slender with dark eyes and smooth skin, was perhaps the most beautiful of the four daughters. She married a man who loved her passionately. But Ida did not return his love. Did she think that, in time, her feelings would change? Or was she simply tired of factory work and felt that marriage was an acceptable alternative? Not unreasonable for a young woman who had been slaving six long days a week producing clothes since she was fourteen. We can only surmise. Like her father who had made unwise choices in marriage, so did she. For some years, she lived unhappily with someone she could not love and grew more ill-tempered as time went on. He husband's strong feelings of affection eventually changed into equally strong feelings of dislike. When their two sons were still young boys, they separated and Ida raised the children by herself. After the boys grew into men, married and started raising their own families, Ida lived alone.

I have a memory of visiting her that I must include at this point. Her boys, now young men, were still living with her. My mother, looking for some respite from her unhappy life would claim that she had to visit her sister, Ida, who conveniently lived very far away, in Los Angeles. She didn't go very often, but, when she did, because of the distance, the slow means of traveling, the expense of the ticket, once she was there my father apparently accepted that fact that she would be staying there for some time, perhaps months. I accompanied her on one of the visits. We must have taken a train from Cleveland, where we lived, to Chicago where we picked up the Pullman that was to take us all the rest of the way to L.A. I shall never forget those hours spent with my mother in the Pullman bunk. I was going on five years old. It was probably the month of April, just before my fifth birthday in May. I remember it must have been April as in L.A. I had the joy of my life: I was a happy, care-free child, looking for Easter eggs in a hunt in the lawn of one of the swank Beverley Hills hotels.

But, getting back to the ride from Chicago. We were cuddled together in the closet-like bunk and my mother opened a navel orange to share. I shall never forget its delicious odor, but what I remember most is that my mother was cheerful and relaxed. My child's intuition — and children we all know are super-sensitive to a parent's moods — sensed that my mother was happy; that, for once, she wasn't tense, fearful, conveying unspoken but constant anxiety to her child. So, of course, I could also relax and be happy.

The Los Angeles visits gave my mother some respite and, at least this one time I went with her, furnished me with some happy times that have remained with me and have nourished me. That egg hunt was one of them. It's hard to describe the blissful experience of being a child, hunting with other children, breathlessly happy at discovering an egg or two (I think they were chocolate). It was a rare occurrence in a dark childhood where tension abounded. As the youngest of four I was not directly affected but, in some intimate part of me, absorbed the sadness and fear of the others. When I see photos of myself in family photos, I see a glum face: not the face of a happy child.

I'll never forget our stay in my aunt's apartment. Her two adult sons dominated the household. They were lords of a sacrosanct spot, a particular room where they spent hours listening to classical records. I begged to be allowed to go in and, after much remonstrance, not wanting to be disturbed by this little kid, they grudgingly permitted me to sit in a corner, if I didn't make a sound, and listen to the music: my first taste of classical music that I instinctively loved and wanted to hear more of. My two cousins, though they put up with me huddling in my corner, decided it was too much to ask to have me at the dinner table. My aunt accommodated and put up a stool, as the table, and a chair, behind the kitchen door, where, hidden from their view, she diligently served me my meals. She became the devoted caregiver as my mother was ill at least part of time we were there.

I'm wondering if, after months of keeping herself together, once in a protective atmosphere, my mother allowed herself to give in, to be taken care of by a kind sister. I remember that Aunt Ida gave her her own bed and slept perhaps on a couch or even on the floor. She was the devoted sister my mother needed to sustain her during the oppressive years of her married life.

When I saw Aunt Ida next, after many years, she had become a difficult elderly woman, in poor health with Parkinson's Disease. My mother, then living in L.A., took care of this sister who, in the past, had helped her through sad times but, after having lived with Ida for a few years and putting up with someone who had become hyper-critical, taking care of her had become too arduous for my mother who was no longer young herself. My aunt's deteriorating physical condition solved the situation. She had to be transferred to a nursing home. On a visit to my mother, during my college years, my mother insisted that I visit my aunt in this depressing establishment full of old sick people. As a young college student, it was not my "cup of tea." But my mother knew Ida needed to feel she was cared for. Now in a position to help, she did what she could to make her sister's last years a pleasant as possible. She never forgot Ida's devotion to her during her own difficult years.

Though we know something about Rose's three sisters, we know very little about the young men in the family. Before we return to the young Rose, still unmarried, let's follow the paths they took. Typical of many immigrant families, the youth of the first generation sought professions that could improve their lot over that of the parents, who, while struggling to keep food on the table, encouraged their children's education. I can start with Harold. I've already mentioned, in passing, that he became a medical doctor. He married an attractive, sharp-witted young woman. Their later years together, however, touched on the tragic. Something else I'll save for later. Jack, the eldest, moved to Canada and presumably made a comfortable living there. I never met him, but my mother related one incident to me that will endear him to me forever. Considering his remark, she must have been relatively young when my uncle paid a visit and (bless him) had the courage to remark to my father—as he surely knew he would be provoking an angry and perhaps violent response: "Look at Rose. The way you're treating her she already looks like an old woman!" After that, Mother said my father never spoke to him. After Jack and Harold, comes Maurice, who became a pharmacist. I never met him either, but I do have a photo of him and a young woman. Mother told me he was passionately in love with that young lady and wanted to marry her but, first, needed to cure his syphilis. Being a pharmacist, he had access to mercury, which was supposed to be a cure. (And for all I know, perhaps it was, in minute amounts.) In any case, he took so much that it killed him. A sad conclusion to what might have been a tender relationship. Another brother, Bob, I know little about except, in an old photo, I see him as a pilot in World War I. Later, in Cleveland, he became part of fashionable, cultured society and had little to do with us who were never part of his social set. For Louie, the brother close in age to Albert, the story is happier than Albert's. He became a lawyer, married, had children and, being a mild natured person—my personal memory of him—was resigned, or perhaps content, with his good-looking, dynamic, but self-serving wife. The adolescent I was could sense this in her character, aside from noting my mother's obvious disapproval of her. Lastly, we have Albert who didn't achieve much of a higher education. Did odd jobs, plumbing and what not. But, for me, with his warmth and affection, he was perfect the way he was. As for the letter my grandfather wrote to this son, Albert, in spite of his writing that it was not easy for him to do it in English, you can see from the following excerpt that at least his written English was very good, the results of someone determined to learn the language. The letter is dated June 6, 1923 and was written when, for unknown reasons, my grandfather was in Los Angeles. I have maintained his spelling and punctuation.

My dear son Albert,

I was realy surprised that finaly I received a letter from you, but it was just in time because I did not have any letters from Cleveland for a long time. I was glad to hear from you, but I felt very sorry too, about your troubles … I will tell you the truth that I worry about it more than you do, well, my dear boy, this is a thing that passed, it can not be helped and we were not able to prevent it even before, therefore, I advise you not to think of it at all, take it out from your mind and think about something else, you can find different enjoyments and different pleasures in your life, especially now when you earn enough for a living and I will send you once in a while a few dollars too, now you will find inclosed a check of $10.00 You shell buy a watch for it, if you have a watch buy a chain for the money or something else. [Some family news follows] I made my letter as brief as possible the reason for it is because I am not free in writing the English language and for the same reason I think it is not necessary for me to write to every one of our family separate it is to much English writing, therefore if you please give my best regards to everyone. [He enumerates all his children and their spouses to whom he sends wishes of good health and happiness.]

Your father, Sigmund Cohn

I never knew my grandfather but, after reading this touching letter where a father searches for ways, inevitably inadequate, to comfort his son, I had a better understanding of my mother's tender feelings for him. Furthermore, as he refers to Albert's "troubles" and encourages him to seek other "enjoyments" and "different pleasures" I'm wondering if the frightful operation didn't take place later in Albert's life, perhaps when he was a young man already earning his living. How can I be sure that it happened when he was thirteen? I have the impression I was told that, but can't be certain, particularly in light of the letter, which I'd read many years ago but have reread with more care. My detective antennae tell me to reconsider what I always thought to be a fact and take into account the letter which, quite convincingly, points to another time in Albert's life. Perhaps, the later operation is a reason for his manly appearance. Perhaps, after all, he was in no need of hormone treatments, either. I wish my sweet uncle were still here though I'd probably not dare to probe for information about such a devastating event. Now that I write about it, I think it's the first time I realize how indeed devastating it must have been, how it unmanned him, especially if it happened when he was a young fellow, thinking about sweethearts and then marriage and children. I only knew him as a kind, sensible human being and, young as I was, gave little thought, then, to his personal drama.

But I must put thoughts of Uncle Albert to rest and go on with Rose's story. When almost twenty, and though girls married at a young age in those days, she was still unmarried. She had had a beau when she was about 16 who was interested in marriage, but she'd decided she was too young to marry. Her sisters and brothers-in-law grew concerned that she would not find a husband, particularly as she seldom left the house. They devised a plan. One day, Esther's husband brought one of his workmen home to meet Rose. The young man was nice-looking and ambitious—one of the hardest-working men that, Esther's husband said, he'd ever employed. I imagine that the young, inexperienced woman was impressed, not only by his looks, but by his polite manner and what her brother-in-law had said about the energy and determination he showed at work. My mother never described this meeting or the "courtship" — though I find it difficult to imagine my father courting — but I imagine she was physically attracted to him and, once more, must have thought this ambitious young man could be trusted to provide for her and the children they might have. So, without knowing him very well, she agreed to a marriage. What were his thoughts? I can only guess that, as my mother was a pretty young woman, he was attracted to her as well. Furthermore he didn't underestimate the value of marrying into his employer's family. No doubt, during those arduous days at work, his mind was active as well. Not having much schooling (at age 14, he left his native Latvia, part of the Russian Empire, for America), he needed to learn from his experience. While at work, he observed, he noted how to run a business, how to supply it, what people to hire. In one of my few conversations with my father — or perhaps I just overheard it — he said that he was terrible as a plumber and that's why he had to learn to organize others to do the hands-on work. I was also told — perhaps by my mother, but I'm unsure — that he knew that her father, my grandfather, had saved a little money. I remember my mother saying that her father would save his money, penny by penny, literally, by not taking the penny-transfer for the tramway up the hill to their house. He saved those pennies, and perhaps others, until she told me he had amassed a fortune: $100! I'm wondering if this was an additional inducement for the fellow to marry the young woman, feeling sure that his future father-in-law would use that sum to help him establish a business. In any case, he was probably thinking that Esther's husband, his future brother-in-law, would help him find his first jobs for the plumbing company he had already decided to organize and build for himself.

My father must have worked long hours, slowly building his plumbing and heating business into one that, after many years, would be one of the most important in the city. The Great Depression had also, ironically, been a boost for him. Aside from any possible family help, his growing business sense helped him see other sources of investment: property. During the Depression people who had a bit of real estate were begging for buyers and weren't asking much of a purchasing price. My father somehow got the few dollars together (did my grandfather's $100 help here?) to buy a number of properties that, in the ensuing years, he sold at a handsome profit, which he could then invest in his company. Eventually, this company — taking on air conditioning in later years — became a solid financial support for the members of the family and, later, created a substantial inheritance to be shared — the source of much conflict, which I mention in passing but, in the telling, would demand yet another story ...

The young wife must have discovered quite early on that this was not going to be a happy marriage. Her husband, my father-to-be, was strong willed and successful in what he set out to do, but that did not mean he was loving or kind. In fact, quite the opposite. The following events that were related to me speak for themselves. Of the four children in the family, only the two older ones, Raymond and Marion, had been born. They were still little. My mother told me that my father would give her just enough money to buy food for them, which she prepared and stored in their modest refrigerator, though at that time it probably was an icebox. My father, however, concerned about saving every penny, would not buy any food for himself when at work. He'd come home in the evening famished and would, without a thought for his children, let alone his wife, eat what my mother was planning to give to her two little ones. I never thought to ask her how she improvised something for them to eat the next day. Another unanswered question of so many I regret not having thought to ask.

The other episode involves a dreaded disease: either whooping cough or scarlet fever for which no vaccinations were available at the time. As with our own coronavirus, the only way of controlling it was by quarantine. One of the children, or perhaps both, had one of those diseases. My mother was strictly quarantined with the two children and a sign was put on the door to ward off visitors. There were no half-way measures: one was made to stay in complete isolation. Not venture out. How to eat? I think my mother and the two children would very nearly have starved if family or neighbors hadn't left food on the doorstep. My father stayed somewhere else. However, it was not important enough for him to leave food for his family. These two episodes in my mother's life as a young mother have remained with me. We see my mother, centered on the survival of her children: my father totally involved in making a place in the outside world. The family was merely a footnote in his life.

When I think of my mother, as a young wife, I can imagine how much she yearned for the love she had felt in her father's house. Even many years later, well into her 90s, she would speak of her father with great affection. As a young wife, she must have remembered her father's gentle manner, his need to reflect and to learn. He was not a successful businessman, as her husband was bound to be one day, but, as we've seen in his letter to Albert, he was kind and ready to console and advise his children. Perhaps she thought too of her brothers and sisters and their hard years together. Yet, throughout those difficult times, there was the solace of companionship.

But now everything was different. Her father, grown older and quite ill, had died when Rose was a young mother. She visited her sisters when she could but still had to return to her own unhappy house. Also, not all of her sisters welcomed her visits. After a youth of hardship and struggle, some, like Fanny, had developed into ungenerous human beings.

We know that Esther, for example, kept clothing and household expenses down to the barest minimum. She was one that was not too pleased to have her sister, Rose, visit regularly. She felt obliged to offer her something to eat—an extra weekend expense. It was only later on in years, however, that, I was told, Esther admitted to these uncomfortable feelings. Esther's husband had died and Esther, herself, was not well. We know that she would call Rose and keep her on the phone for hours with myriad complaints. Rose realized that Esther was lonely and because she, herself, wanted to escape her own house, decided to visit Esther every Saturday with Albert, their youngest brother. We know that Albert remained unmarried but was fond of visiting his sisters. He also wanted to help Esther through this difficult period. But Esther, even though she was pleased to see her brother and sister, became irritated at the little meal they ate together. One day she burst out in anger and Rose, very much offended, did not come the next Saturday, nor did Albert. Of course, Rose did eventually visit again, but she remembered to bring her own food. The Saturday visits were no longer the happy time they had been for Rose.

My vision of my mother as a victim of the stressful years of her marriage where her only resources were visits to her sisters', like the ones to Esther or the more lengthy ones to Ida in California—or, as we shall see, retreats into illness—are mitigated by other memories I have—or rather experiences she related that convey an energy and initiative as a young adult, which over the years, would help her survive.

One experience was an adventure she had when she was 16 years old. No doubt wanting another kind of life than caring for a household and her younger siblings, she decided to join her eldest brother who was married and, we know, lived in Canada.

I never knew how she had the means to travel. She didn't work outside of the home like her sisters and would have had to ask them—who had little money themselves—or her father, who had barely enough to support the household—for the bus fare. On the other hand, she may have been free to leave as the aunt her father married after her mother died was probably there to keep things going. There are, unfortunately, blanks in the story of my mother's life and so I'm left, once again, to reconstruct the narrative. We know that her eldest brother, once she was married, was concerned about her welfare. In fact his reprimanding my father is the only instance of any of my mother's siblings standing defiantly by her side during those sad years. One would think, therefore, that Jack had tender feelings for his little sister and might very well have invited her, as a 16-year-old, to visit him and his wife in Canada and, to enable her to come, have sent her the bus fare. It's beyond belief that she would have simply packed up and left without an invitation. Furthermore, she would have had to have permission from her father who was probably not the authoritarian her own mother might well have been to manage the large household but, nevertheless, she needed his assent to feel at ease about going so far away. If it were to visit her brother and, furthermore, at the brother's expense, I imagine her father would see no reason to object.

My mother related that she made the trip with her little "satchel" and stayed with her brother and sister-in-law for how long? Several weeks? In any event, at some point the sister-in-law no longer wanted this young girl hanging around the household and insisted she leave. Her brother conceded to his wife's demands and my mother returned to Cleveland, her adventure at an end. But what gumption it must have taken for this young girl, who probably didn't know Jack that well, having had little contact with the eldest in the family, who had never traveled on her own, perhaps never set foot in a train or a long distance bus, to decide to go to another country and, even though we surmise she was invited, not knowing quite what to expect when she got there. It revealed energy and ingenuity. I imagine the young girl jumping at the opportunity to live a more exciting life than one in her poor household where, since she had been taken out of school, she spent her days. It didn't work but she never expressed regret. She'd seized the opportunity to see a bit of the world.

Another experience my mother described to me is one of regret. Perhaps, in hindsight, her decision was the wrong one but it resulted from her desire to shape her own life. She was not much older than the 16-year-old who went to Canada. I've already mentioned that, before she was introduced to my father, there was a young man who had fallen in love with her and wanted to marry her but, as we saw from her decision to venture out and go to Canada, she was spirited and wasn't ready to marry and settle down. And so, when her beau proposed marriage, not prepared to change one household for another, she rejected his proposal. She wanted more from life than the household tasks she'd assumed since she was a child. He must have eventually gone on his way.

A few years later, at 19, we see her faced with the possibility of marriage once again, and she made what turned out to be another mistake. But, ready at last to accept marriage, how could she anticipate that her union with the young man, who seemed personable and capable and whom, once more, her family recommended to her, would be the source of many years of unhappiness? Unfortunately, she made the decision that locked her into a relationship, without the compensation of love or companionship that she was seeking.

And so life with my father began. After the first two children, were born, my father brought his elderly mother over from Europe to help out. She could see the unhappiness he was creating in his household, but, as she depended on him, was fearful of criticizing him. However, my mother said, she did what she could to help by looking after the children. It gave my mother some respite allowing her to now and then get out of the house for a walk. On one such outing she saw a couple approaching from a distance and recognized her former beau — who just a few years back had proposed marriage to her — now with his arm around the waist of his girlfriend: the image of a couple in love. My mother hid in the recess of a building where she could not be seen. She looked at them and realized that she could have been that young woman in the embrace of the young man. She was heartsick at what she had foolishly given up. When they went by, she went home to what she knew was waiting for her.

My father's mother, a woman of little education or worldly experience, must have stayed on for quite some time, though I have no idea for how long. Nor do I know when or where she died: in the States? or did my father ship her back before that. But I have good feelings for this simple woman who befriended her daughter-in-law, had compassion for her, in a time of great need.

My mother did indeed endure years of unhappiness, victim of my father's harshness, his frightening dominance, his lack of respect for her but in taking a long view of my mother's life, I recognize more and more clearly her survival techniques that helped her last until her elderly years when, with my father's death, she could at last enjoy her freedom. She was unable to confront him and fight openly for her identity. She had to find other ways of keeping herself together, of convincing herself that she had value. How did she do it? One indication of her resourcefulness was her decision to save pennies from the allowance her husband gave her and to pay a professional photographer to take photos of her. She discovered a way to exist, to have an identity, if only in the eyes of the photographer who, albeit for a sum, gave her his undivided attention, taking great care in posing her. I have two of the photos, and I suspect there were more: in one, the photographer has dressed her up as a young Chinese woman. She smiles shyly out to us—or rather at the photographer—apparently pleased at the opportunity to play a role. In the other she is dressed elegantly, her hair is curled, and she's wearing what was probably her best black dress, with a string of beads around her neck. The photographer has obviously put thought into the composition: she is sitting in a chair, against a romantic background of hazy trees and water. Her legs are crossed; her chin leans pensively on her hand, her arm supported on the arm of the chair—an ornate object with lion heads ending each arm rest. She has a sweet smile and looks relaxed and happy with the world. She went to the photographer's studio with a mission: to be recognized as a person by someone, and it would have had to be done in secret and with careful planning so as not to be discovered. (Did she share the photos with her sisters? I doubt it as one of them might have carelessly exposed the truth.) During the taking of the photo—a lengthy, complicated procedure—she was looked at, dressed especially for the occasion, artfully posed, and for the time the experience lasted (and that she could relive looking at the photo) she existed! She was a victim in her marriage but, with a strong desire to live, was resourceful enough to survive over the years of trial.

Something else that I'm beginning to think of as a kind of survival strategy was her escape into sickness.

When I was eight years old, and why I distinctly remember my age is a mystery to me, my mother took to her bed. She fell into a deep depression, refusing to eat. I'd been a sick child with surges of bronchitis (or was it pneumonia? I was never told) but I undoubtedly frightened everyone by my sieges of uncontrollable coughing. (I remember my father saying, probably not meaning it, but, nevertheless, menacing enough for me to remember it to this day: "Let her die already!") And I was also what you might call a "cry baby," whining and needy: a burden I thought to my mother who I realized was unhappy enough without my adding to her cares. So, quite naturally, I assumed that her illness was my fault. I remember going into the bathroom and deciding that I was the culprit. Why the decision was made in a bathroom? Considering it now after all these years, perhaps because it was a private place where one could make solemn decisions. I realized my mother was seriously ill, but with a sickness that mystified me, and my 8-year-old mind had to find a reason for it. It was clear to me: I was at fault, and I had no way of helping her. My father and my older sister took charge of the household. Though this sister had my father's skinflint nature, they must have been frightened by my mother's condition and they both consented to have a nurse take care of my mother, who, I believe, saved her life by, with an ingenious suggestion, inducing her to eat. She told my mother to chew the meat on her plate and just swallow the juice and spit out the rest if she couldn't get it down. Writing eighty years later, I'm not sure how I know this. My mother must have related to me though I can't remember when. Be that as it may, this unusual advice that kept my mother alive has remained a lasting part of my childhood memories.

In bed, she was depressed, unhappy, but she was protected by her illness. She was safe. She could close her eyes, no longer have to shore herself up each day to face her fear and repulsion for a man she, finally, could think of no other way to escape. A dangerous mechanism for surviving a hateful life. She could have ended it but, deep in her, she must have wanted to go on. Also she was responsive to the nurse's attentions. Was it like the photographer who attended to her, fussing over her with the proper background for the photo, the right posture, the manner of dressing, all for her? Here, in a life or death circumstance, someone wanted to save her, thought her valuable enough for that. It must have touched that survival impulse in her that we've seen at other times in her troubled life. So, indeed, she survived to live on for some more unhappy years with my father and, in fact, in her sixties, outlived him. A success story, of sorts.

Now, back to the other sisters, as adults. We've learned that Fanny had never been kind to Rose. As years went on, as we've seen, she proved to be harmful to her youngest sister. Fanny was capable and educated and had a strong personality that could influence others. My father respected the educated and the successful and he listened to what Fanny had to say. She could have urged him, for example, to control his bad temper, to be less harsh with the children, more considerate of Rose's feelings. Instead, as we've noted before, she liked to describe what she felt were Rose's weaknesses and comparing herself to her sister, was able to tarnish the image my father had of his wife. After a visit with Fanny, Rose's husband was more angry and unkind than ever. I've noted elsewhere that my father would even repeat to my mother what her sister had said, using Fanny's comments to reproach her. My mother didn't need any other proof of Fanny's behavior. In fact, I ask myself why I seem to dwell on my Aunt Fanny in my "mother's story." She was, however, a fixture in my mother's life and, though she could be a menace, she was also captivating and creative. At some point in her life, she gave up nursing and opened a costume shop with fabulous, extravagant costumes of elegant materials, many or all of which she made herself. I remember wandering in and out among the costumes as a child, brushing my face against the brocade, running my hands over the long sleeves and sweep of the gowns. It was a fairyland for me, moments of delicious escape for me from the tensions of my home, just as her visits to our house, in spite of her at times insidious behavior, probably brought some entertaining moments to my mother's dour existence.

From among her sisters, only Ida was a real comfort. When she still lived in Cleveland, she came to visit Rose often. Frequently she'd find her sister discouraged with no energy to take care of her house and children. Mother said Ida would help prepare dinner and bathe the children. (This was in the years before I, the fourth child, was born.) It must have been a great comfort to my mother to have Ida with her. She knew that she was with someone who loved her, a dear sister, who, in spite of her ill-tempered moments, was to be cherished.

Except for Albert, Rose didn't see much of her brothers. Jack was a good deal older and, as we've seen, lived far away, working and creating his own family. I think Bob was next in line. We know he was a pilot in World War I—and I'm sure he had stories to tell about what flying, especially in war time, was like in those days. Alas, I can't pass anything on. I'm quite sure he made a comfortable living though I don't know how, and that he sent his sons to college. I've mentioned that he and his family lived in a different, and what would have been considered, a more prestigious social sphere than my parents, who had little formal education or what my Uncle Bob would have considered "culture." If he had found our household up to his standards, he would surely have visited our house on occasion. However, I do know this much about him: that he was considered something of a "snob." Who exactly conveyed that message to me? It simply hung in the air, so to speak, ready for a child to pick up.

Harold became a doctor—how he paid for his studies is a mystery to me. In the 1920s, education cost less, but he assuredly had to work and study at the same time to pay, what for him, must have been a sizable sum. As for Maurice, the pharmacist, we know his life ended tragically. Harold's late years were close to tragic as well. He had married Marie, an attractive woman with a keen mind. He was madly in love with her—I still have one of his letters, along with the letter by my grandfather—and, in spite of her not being Jewish, they married. I must add here that not only Harold but Jack married women who were not Jewish. Now, one thinks nothing of such marriages—outside of those who are devout Jews—but then the social pressure would have discouraged such unions. My guess is that the two men had grown up to think independently and had their father as an example: one who respected learning but, as my mother often said with pride, was not "religious," as if being devout would be a kind of flaw in one's character. Coming from a closed in Jewish community in Minsk, I can see that my grandfather, his "nose always in books," as his wife said, felt that conformity to religious practice was a limitation. I would guess that he associated it with those he considered basically uneducated, in spite of their devotion to religious texts. Their house may have been one of the few secular ones in the Jewish enclave. In any event, I suspect that this attitude had an effect on his two sons who followed their passion regardless of what society would say.

So, Harold married his love. In his letter dated the 26th of March 1913, of which I have a copy, Harold writes to Fanny—who had just left her children to run off with the man she loved and so could be understanding of Harold's passionate involvement with a woman he hopes to marry—of his anguish over what he has just learned. Here is an excerpt expressing his turbulent emotions in his own intense language:

> … the story she told me sounded like fiction. Your life story placed on the side of hers would look like a heaven compared to a hell. I sat there and listened to her changing all colors under the rainbow: I trembled like a leaf; I felt the floor give way under me; my eyes turned glassy but shed no tears, for they were frozen with the cool, clammy sensation of my body and overburdened heart; my head was swimming and my heart was pounding for she concluded her story with the shocking news that she probably (but I am sure it's definitely) will <u>never be able to bear children</u>. I know not whether such news would

affect others; nor am I sure that even you can realize what it means. But you do know that I love children, and what such a condition would mean to me; for even as I write this now it brings tears to my eyes ... Here then is the source of all my troubles: knowing my <u>love</u> for <u>children</u>, and knowing my love for her, will I be happy with her, or will I not be? My idea is that I will be both <u>unhappy with her</u> and <u>unhappy</u> if I am <u>without her</u> ... [The underlining is his.]

Harold entered into this marriage with his beloved who would never be able to bear children. It was a wrenching conflict for him. I wasn't around in their younger years, when, in spite of their childlessness, they surely had some good times together where they enjoyed common interests and companionship, but I was a close observer of them later on when they lived in a huge old house my father had bought in Cleveland Heights. (My father was very conscious of how he was considered outside of his home—never mind what went on inside—and this big house, which was considered a "mansion," was impressive.) My Aunt Marie had become an interior decorator and my father hired her to create drapes and other decorations to enhance the house. Part of the payment, I understood, was that my uncle and aunt could lodge in our house while she was doing the work. I remember a skeletally thin woman, moving slowly, painfully with two crutches down our long, elegant stairway, surely a deadly challenge for her. In spite of her physical condition, her face, with its fine, aquiline features, was still remarkable, remains of what must have been her striking looks as a young woman. And what a mind! I remember her quips, her sharp rejoinders; I don't remember the content, mainly the rapidity and conciseness of the response. There is one thing she said, however, that I shall never forget. My father often ate alone. We'd serve him his food at our large dining table and, as often as we could, would then retire to the kitchen to not have to keep him company. One late afternoon, Aunt Marie came into the room, looked at my father, and off to the side—he wouldn't have been able to hear—said: "He eats like an animal!" Not quite true. His eating habits were quite acceptable but it was an outburst conveying her repulsion, her utter dislike of the man for whom she was working. I never could have expressed myself so openly. Her remarks served an inner need, and I remember them to this day with a kind of smug satisfaction. When one can express a repressed feeling, even via someone else's words, it offers a moment of silent happiness.

But I am wandering from Uncle Harold's story. His wife was wracked with pain, perhaps from severe arthritis, and she grew dependent on morphine to help her cope with the condition. At first Harold could prescribe the morphine but I imagine that he couldn't keep prescribing ad infinitum and thus had to beg his colleagues, his medical friends, to do the prescribing. It was horrendous: a burden of shame that would never end as long as his wife was alive. He was forced, week after week, to solicit prescriptions of morphine, or perhaps find some other way of procuring it. I'll never know. But I do know that this great love—though sadly for them both, a childless marriage—turned into a bitter, resentful relationship as Harold was forced, because of his wife's needs, into a life of humiliation. Where and when they both died, I have no idea. My last picture of them is my aunt on her crutches and my uncle's somber face.

Heart disease ran in my mother's family, though she was spared. First Fanny, then Esther, then two of her brothers, including her beloved Albert, were victims of a weak heart. Then my father, too strong and healthy to have need of a doctor became ill and, after a year of suffering, died of prostate cancer. My mother took care of her husband and tried to make his last days as comfortable as she could. I have to imagine how she felt tending to my father whom she must have feared and disliked for many years of their marriage. Now he was the weak one who needed her and she measured up to the hardship of caring for his sick body. The irony of it all was that finally my father appreciated her! At last, but much too late, he was thankful for her gentle care and responded to her with the consideration and respect he had not been able to show during their long life together.

After my father's death, my mother was at last free to live as she pleased. The hard years of her married life had taken a toll on her physical strength but, actually, outside of extreme high blood pressure (which she refused to medicate) she was basically healthy and, once more, had a strong desire to enjoy whatever years remained to her. Also, she was financially untroubled, as my father had left a wealthy estate behind him. Here I could diverge into the unpleasant chapter of certain family members attempts to control the money, giving my mother an "allowance" until she was 85, at which time she was supposed to have reached the end of her life and would no longer need financial support. As my mother lived until just a few months before her 97th birthday, she would have been an indigent for some years if these individuals had had their way. Fortunately, my brother, Raymond, came to the rescue, hiring a lawyer that protected my mother's interests. And so, yes, she could live comfortably. But it could have ended otherwise.

My mother's choice to live in California was not a surprise for anyone. It was there she had enjoyed happy escapades from her unfortunate marriage. The clement weather around Los Angeles was another factor, to be sure, but the main attraction was being with Ida, her only remaining sister and her dearest. We remember how kind Ida had been to my mother in their younger years. I've noted that as an elderly woman, however, she had become overly critical, superstitious of others, even those, like my mother, who wanted to help her. In short, she was no fun to live with. She and her husband had been separated for many years, and her two grown sons—the ones who didn't want me at their table—avoided their mother as much as they could. I think we can understand why, though being as they were, they might very well have neglected their mother for other reasons.

My mother continued to live in Santa Monica for some years. She created a life for herself, a solitary one, where she engaged various helpers who became friends of a sort. Now, at the vantage of my own age of 88, living alone in the midst of the coronavirus crisis, I have a new-found respect for my mother's capabilities. She didn't have the advantage of an education and an active cultural life to fill her days, but, with her sensitivity to people and the appreciation of the beauty of her natural surroundings along the ocean where she lived, she composed her daily life, interspersed with, I'm ashamed to say, my infrequent visits, as well as those of my siblings, as we were all involved with our own lives.

It was probably after the death of Ida when my mother was no longer occupied with concerns over her sister's well-being that the need to see me must have become overwhelming. My husband and I were in Paris enjoying one of his sabbaticals. The children were, I believe, 12 and 14. We were involved in their education and our own busy Paris life, when, to my astonishment, I received the only letter my mother ever wrote to me. (Normally I would call her to find out how she was.) This letter was carefully written in a script she'd learned as a child but, as an adult, I'm sure had had few occasions to use. In it, she told me how much she missed me and that I should think about visiting her more often. I know she must have labored over the letter to express her feelings of loneliness convincingly but, still, with decorum. It also involved her swallowing her pride to ask for a daughter's visit, when the visits should have been forthcoming without any requests needed! I was much affected by the letter. It was obvious she was in great need to see me or she would never have composed such a letter. I realized that, indeed, I had been too taken up with my own life and had neglected her. From then on, I started visiting my mother regularly, at least every other month, going from France (if we were on a sabbatical or in a house in southern France we eventually purchased) to California if need be. Her letter was a call to attention and I'm glad to this day that she took the brave initiative to write it.

During my visits to California, I had occasion to appreciate my mother's sense of aesthetics. I was aware of this seemingly instinctive love of the harmonious, the beautiful. It showed in her desire to have paintings to decorate her apartment, but paintings with "old world" quality that resembled museum works. She wanted to enjoy looking at them but, from lessons learned during her early years of poverty and marriage to my father, the enjoyment could not be had at an exorbitant price. This led to a wonderful time together scouring numerous antique shops in our hunt for the right paintings at an acceptable price. We actually found a few very nicely done works, one in fact by a well-known California painter that was greatly undervalued by the antique dealer. It is now hanging on one of my walls, reminding me of the fun we had together sharing our interest in works of art and having the satisfaction of finding some she would make a part of her life.

I'm reminded that, indeed, this sense of aesthetics was a part of her even before my father's death. For example, she had great pleasure picking out the right combination of clothes, looking for a harmony, a touch of elegance in the white color of a simple blouse perhaps setting off the shape of the jacket top. When my dear friend from college, Diane Vreuls, came to visit me in Cleveland after our graduation from the University of Wisconsin, my mother was quick to appreciate the quiet elegance in Diane's clothes that she valued in her own. She didn't need or want to spend a lot of money on fancy name garments: she was searching for the delight of a "look" that appealed to her sense of harmony that was, I know not how or why, natural to her. Perhaps she was searching for pleasure denied her in life: the simple joy of perceiving beauty, whether in nature, in clothes, or even in the sophisticated realm of art.

It was to help my mother enter this sophisticated world that, on the few occasions she visited us in our home in Rockland County, we would, rather hesitantly, take her to the Metropolitan Museum. She was elderly and was bound to fatigue easily by the multitude of art pieces, and I was afraid she would be overwhelmed by the experience. However, knowing she loved to look at paintings, I wanted to give her the exposure to the richness of museum collections that she'd never enjoyed in her hard life. To my surprise and delight, we spent at least one or two hours in the museum without any apparent fatigue on her part, though, looking back, she may have been putting on a good show to not spoil the occasion. In any event, she was attentive to the beauty around her and seemed to take in the brief remarks I made about the paintings, giving her a little insight or information but not so much that it would detract from the simple pleasure of looking at the works.

Another activity my mother and I shared during my visits to California after my father's death was deciding on donations. She wanted to help those in need and liked the idea of supporting education, protecting nature, and other worthy causes. And of course she got a lot of requests for donations, which we would go through meticulously. Reading the brochures to her and weighing whom to give to and how much was a tedious process, taking quite a bit of time as my mother carefully questioned me on the value, as I saw it, of each request. My mother was in a better financial situation than I by far. However, by reading over the material and helping her make a choice I could contribute, if not my own money, at least with the many hours of sorting and deciding and hopefully intelligent advice. In the process I became familiar with a host of Native American associations and other groups that, at the present moment, now financially comfortable, are part of my own list of worthy associations. It's truly a kind of continuation of my life with mother.

It took my mother's letter to start my routine of regular visits. In contrast, my brother didn't need to be encouraged to stop in to see our mother. His children were grown; he was free to go to the West Coast, a region where he loved to vacation, and, while he was in the L.A. area, it was an opportune moment to see mother. But I also think his attachment to her motivated his visits, though he never overtly expressed those feelings. When her son came to see her, it was, I'm sure, a very special time for my mother. I'm convinced that outside of the beau she had as a young girl, my brother was "the man in her life." When I saw them together in those years, I sensed their unspoken understanding of each other. In fact, they have a history together which should be related, showing not only my mother's love for her son, but her resourcefulness.

My brother, Raymond, was, as I've noted, the eldest and the only boy, my mother's only son. He resembled her in looks and character: gentle, refined, also fearful, dominated and humiliated by my father. When Pearl Harbor struck he was among the first to enlist: an acceptable – and to others, admirable – way of escaping.

Before that, my mother did all in her power to protect him. She was his ally and he was, in a way, her companion. I remember her telling me that they took singing lessons together! (My father did have some normal Jewish father's reflexes: I think music lessons were part of that. He paid for my piano lessons as well.)

Mentioning the singing lessons brings up an image that, otherwise, would not have occurred to me. I recall, now, that my mother would often sing softly to herself as she busied herself in the kitchen. I remember her soft voice holding a tune very nicely, singing "old fashioned" romantic songs she must have heard in her younger days, like "The last rose of summer" — my guess at the title of one of the songs she favored. I sensed that the singing helped keep up her spirits, along with the pleasure she might have had in remembering the song. The kitchen singing — years after the time of her singing lessons — links her to the time before I was born and to behavior — actually taking lessons — that was unlike the downcast mother to whom I was accustomed. Still young and, I would guess, with the energy and ambition of a younger person, she must have convinced my father that two could take a lesson for the price of one. Or perhaps that was actually true! I'll never know, but lessons, there were. With her need to be with her son and the joy of sharing an experience with him, she must also have had some confidence in her voice, feeling she was capable of measuring up to the challenge of instruction. Here's another small discovery about my mother of particular appeal to me because of the place of music in my own life. If my mother, with her ear for singing, had had guidance as a youngster to develop her facility, what would she have been capable of? A futile question, perhaps, but I can't help posing it.

After this detour, let us return to my brother and an important part my mother played during his college years. Aside from lessons, father paid for his college as a young adult. I think having educated children was part of a tradition and also bolstered his own ego. In any event, he did pay for college, though the expenses, at that time, weren't what they are today and, besides, my brother went to Ohio State University, which would have been economical. Be that as it may, Raymond was not at college to study. He'd gotten away from his sad home and wanted to have a good time, which meant girls and gambling! That's where my mother's thrift was particularly crucial. As

I got older, I was aware of a little purse deep in my mother's closet where she hid away her savings. (I remember looking in my mother's drawers, just looking, finding solace in how her neat drawers reflected her person. I must have snooped in her closet with the same fixation.) However, my brother was not a successful gambler. Few people are. And he had debts. He also impregnated a fellow student and, at that time, almost nothing was more shameful. How to pay his debts and, in addition, pay for an abortion (clandestine, of course)! My mother came to the rescue of her dear son. She dipped into her little purse and pulled out enough money to help him. How she had managed to put aside so much from her allowance, without my father's knowing, is astonishing. It attests to her cleverness motivated by what I now keenly realize was the behavior of a survivor. Money meant she had a measure of power, and that meant conniving ways of, every week, putting a sum away. It allowed her to act. She could, on her own, help her son out of his self-made predicaments. I'm sure she was not proud of his gambling and romantic complications, but here again, though incapable of leaving a bad marriage (you'd have to be an "Aunt Fanny" to have the pluck to do it at that time) I see her capable of the kind of action that helped her prevail: this time it was to help her son, a part of her, to survive as well.

As I said, my brother was like a companion for my mother. I remember when he was in the army and on furlough, he invited her to drive to Los Angeles with him. I presume her excuse was to visit Aunt Ida and, for my father, if she were driven, he'd avoid the expense of a train ticket. So she went and, I could see on her face, how happy she was. However, it was not a happy time for me. I was sick in bed with a strep throat, and no penicillin at the time. I remember my mother telling me how bad she felt leaving me but that I would understand. I had already become something of a moral support for her, so, what could I say? I said what she wanted me to say, but I felt abandoned. My older sisters were there, but I needed my mother. I said I understood, so that she could go with a light heart.

In later years, in California, she wanted my brother's visits — so precious to her — to be as pleasant as possible. She told me that when they took walks together and she could see how much he was enjoying the walk, she was too proud to admit fatigue and so she'd stop now and then and call their attention to an interesting building or some lovely flowers in the park, something that would make them stop a moment so that she could catch her breath: it would seem a natural pause to their vigorous walking.

As I write this, I'm beginning to see my mother differently. The clever strategy she devised to prevent the effects of age from spoiling an enjoyable experience with her son, reminds me of other occasions in her past. She was an unhappy victim of my father's harshness. True enough. But underneath her sadness was a strength invisible to me. How could I perceive that somewhere in her was that hardy 11-year-old determined to measure up to the demands put on her; the intrepid 16-year-old embarking on an adventure in Canada; the young woman who surreptitiously paid for her photo portraits; the mother who, in secret and at great risk if her action were discovered, helped her son get out of deep trouble; the wife who fell into a deep depression but who emerged from it, nevertheless, with a helping hand from her nurse and in response to someone who seemed genuinely to care if she healed? She came back to life because, in spite of all, she had a strong desire to live. Only now, looking back on her life, do I realize that the image of my mother as a helpless victim was sorely limited. What was essential — her ingenuity, her resilience — was missing.

As we've seen, my mother's life did not end at 85, per the program of certain individuals. She did, however, have very high blood pressure and was stubborn in her refusal to medicate. But vitamins were "natural," as opposed to medication, and she was convinced, along with many others, that taking an assortment of them promoted good health. A vitamin "doctor" was recommended and she spent many hours, and money, consulting with him. I don't know how helpful the vitamins were but her interest in their health benefits and the consultations with this person kept her occupied, and that, in itself, served a purpose for someone living alone.

As for her high blood pressure, on my visits I would plead with her to take the medicine, used by many, and for many years, to lower it. In fact, one day, a gentleman was waiting, as we were, for the elevator in her apartment building. One side of his body was paralyzed. He had a crutch or a walker, I can't remember, but I do remember discreetly pointing him out to my mother and warning her that that could happen to her if she were not reasonable. Indeed, in time, that is exactly what happened. When about ninety, during a visit to my sister, Helen, in Cleveland, I received a phone call in France where I was participating in a music course and heard the terrible news that my mother had had a stroke. I think I finished the week's session, as my sister said that my rushing back wouldn't change anything. In any event, I was back in Cleveland in short order and found my mother with one side, the left, paralyzed. Thankfully her mind was not affected. It was out of the question for her to continue living in California by herself. The best solution was to find her a nice apartment in the retirement complex in Florida where my sister and her husband spent most of the year. And that's where we settled her and where I found some reliable people to take care of her. After various combinations of helpers who didn't get along with each other, I finally found two who made up a congenial working team. And this leads us into another chapter of my mother's story.

The two women complemented each other: one was an

American woman, competent, a good organizer and ready to take on responsibility. I think she was fond of my mother but my mother, with her keen intuition, could sense that the driving motive of this woman was to make money. However, we needed her and she was ready to do a good job, for the money. The other helper was a woman from Thailand, who spoke excellent English but who could not write it and so was unable to take notes when a doctor would call or whenever else it was necessary. It was a handicap but the other helper compensated. The Thai helper was a precious one, however. She loved my mother, growing more and more attached to her as the months and years went by. Of course, my mother felt her love and warmed to her. I'll call her Sue. She would tell my mother her love troubles. In fact, Sue claimed my mother was her psychiatrist, because of the attentive listening and the helpful advice she gave her. Sue must have filled the long hours they spent together with tales of her love problems. She was in a stable relationship with a man, her "husband" but madly in love with another man. For some reason—perhaps from fear of what he, with his jealous nature, might do—she didn't break with her companion. She no doubt filled my mother's ears with her marital woes and must have asked my mother if she could receive her lover in my mother's apartment, in the second bedroom she used when it was her part of the week to tend my mother. One day—it was bound to happen—the other helper, the morning she was supposed to take over my mother's care, came upon Sue, naked, with her boyfriend still in bed. On my next visit, the helper sat me down with a grave face and related what she'd seen. It was imperative that I tell my mother; after all, it was her house and my mother, in spite of being in a wheel chair after her stroke, made it clear that she was still the mistress of her household. I was unaware, at that point, that my mother had given her permission. Consequently, with some trepidation, I did indeed share the information with her and, to my astonishment, she said that, of course, she knew all about it. Sue was in love with the man and she was happy to help her be with someone she loved. And then she added something that broke my heart. Very matter-of-factly, she said that no one had ever loved her. At least she could help someone else, dear to her, enjoy love—or words to that effect. My mother had learned many things from her unhappy life, among them the importance of loving relationships. People like Sue would value her wisdom and compassion.

Pondering that, it takes me back to an earlier time when a youngster my age recognized those special qualities in my mother. We must have been 13 or 14. My friend was one of the smartest in the class and came from a cultured family. Her father had the first chair of one of the sections of the Cleveland Orchestra. But the parents had marital problems and my friend was deeply disturbed. One day she asked me if she could talk to my mother. She needed her advice. I was surprised but flattered that one of the stars of the class would value my mother's advice to that extent. She hardly knew my mother who, when I had friends in the house, was often in bed. (Being in bed, not "feeling well" continued, I believe, to give my mother a sense of protection, though she never fell into the depression of her earlier years.) In fact, other mothers would frequently take over our kitchen to help make the food for the gatherings. Nevertheless, the little she saw of her must have touched her and motivated her request. My mother accepted the proposal quite naturally, which also surprised me. Accustomed to coping with unhappiness in her marital relationship, or perhaps relying on her experience dealing with the needs of four children, she must have been confident in her ability to understand distress in others, in this case in an adolescent, and be of help. The two of them then retired to a room to have a long talk. My mother, quite rightly, never told me what transpired, but oh I wish she had! I'd love to know what advice my mother came up with to help deal with my friend's anguish. I am left with the realization that my friend sensed my mother was special, the wise counselor that Sue appreciated many years later.

As I write, I realize that I should not have been surprised my friend was convinced my mother would be a good listener to her problems. (Even if my mother could not find a solution, my friend, by verbalizing her woes to a sympathetic person, would lighten the solitary burden she was carrying.) My mother was also an attentive listener to my hopes and school strivings. I remember telling her about the outstanding students in (I think it was) my sixth grade class, and that I was determined to be their friends. I see how her simple listening gave value to me and to my childhood aspirations. Looking back on these occasions, after many years have passed, I have a new appreciation of my mother's gifts.

My mother's ability to empathize is what made her a good listener, but, like any human being, she could also make mistakes. On rare occasions, she would lose her patience with me. (I was prone to colds and went out unbuttoned, unprotected, to her great exasperation as it was she who would have to nurse me through a bad cold I was sure to catch.) But if she allowed herself to reprimand me too harshly—I don't remember her ever slapping me though she came close to it as I tried her patience mightily—she must have felt that she frightened me undeservedly and would apologize. I remember being very proud of my mother who was able to humble herself with an apology to her daughter. Young as I was, I recognized that it was unusual in parents—especially of her generation.

Here, I must introduce another keen memory from my early college years of what would appear to others as an ordinary event but which gave me an image of my mother, which surprised and impressed me. We had already lived in the old mansion for some time. My mother had occasional helpers, my father realizing that keeping up such a large house as elegantly as he required was really too much for her to handle alone. One of the cleaning ladies was Hungarian. Mother was trying her out for the day, but the lady spoke no English! How to communicate? I could hardly believe my ears. I heard my mother speaking Yiddish, which neither she nor my father ever spoke at home — my father did occasionally on the phone with old friends, but that was all as, in my youth, foreign born parents tried to keep an English speaking household for the benefit of the children, with the unfortunate outcome of the offspring rarely acquiring the parents' maternal language. My mother had probably not spoken Yiddish since her childhood or, possibly, her adolescence. I have the feeling that her father would have made every attempt to speak English at home out of the need to master the language, for him and his children. Be that as it may, I knew my mother hadn't used Yiddish for many years. And there she was, gathering up whatever she could remember of the language to communicate to the lady who, in turn, responded in German, a language that was not her principle one either, but which enabled her to understood Yiddish, a German dialect. My mother, though never having studied German, apparently understood the lady, using her ingenuity and memories of past use of Yiddish, a language close enough to standard German (but with many differences) in a way I, the educated college student, with, once more, a passion for language learning, couldn't have. I was terribly proud of my mother seeing her, on this rare occasion, as someone different, more competent, than the vision I had of her, the oppressed victim of a bad marriage. In that incident, I now recognize the resourceful person who is, for me, emerging from the past.

Thinking over this time when I heard my mother speak Yiddish, I suddenly remember one other time when she used Yiddish: it was when she was helping me pack before I left for college. She sang a sad, nostalgic Yiddish song, almost under her breath as if she were singing to herself. I could catch that it was a mother's lament, either singing to her child or singing about her child. The song touched me but I didn't linger over my feelings. I was terribly excited by the thought of escaping the house and starting a new life in college. Only now do I realize how the song revealed my mother's deep sadness anticipating what would be my absence for some months. I heard that same sadness when graduating from Wisconsin, and still at Madison, I entertained the idea of staying on there for graduate work: an acceptable rational for not having to return home. When I called my mother from Madison and heard my mother's anxious, "Oh no!" I realized how devastated she would be (she may have been counting the days until my return) and I quickly backed down. It was at these moments that I had a flash of realization of my mother's needs, but I was young and constructing my life and knew that, though I had to return to Cleveland then to give moral support to my mother, I would one day leave to be on my own. When, a few months later, she managed another trip to visit Ida, I knew it was time for me to leave and I headed to New York City.

Embarking on this reminiscence of my mother's life, I had no idea what I was to discover. Aside from documenting events in the life of an immigrant family from the early 20th century, which in itself is of human interest, I felt that in retelling her life, along with the members of her family who had a part in it, I would be preserving memories of a grandmother and great-grandmother, creating a document for my children and grandchildren of a life that would link them to a long ago family history, which, once I was gone, would be lost. However as the memories and the anecdotes from the past unfolded, I was confronted with more than the ill, unhappy woman I knew as my mother and whose life I intended to evoke. Now, as my story concludes, I see someone with special strengths that, in the past, I, and others, never fully recognized.

Epilog

BUT wait. There is still another story to tell: the one about my father. He caused my mother's unhappiness and created an atmosphere of fear, of constant anxiety that, as a child, affected me as well. Now, at a distance of decades, I recognize that looking upon him as the villain of the story is too simple. He had his own story of survival in a hard world, escaping either inscription or a pogrom in Europe at age 14, and coming to America alone. How he managed that against great odds is, I'm sure, a tale that, unfortunately, I never wanted to ask about and no one else is alive to tell. If told, it might help explain how the young boy of 14 turned out to be the "bad man" in my mother's story.

Still, he was a father and I think, as human beings, we all yearn to have a mother and father figure who will love us and give us a sense of our own value and identity so that when we go out in the world, on our own, we have an idea of who we are and how we can relate to others.

Sadly, the memories I have of my father are of a stony-faced, unsmiling person, someone who provoked fear and distress. However, I do remember one specific episode that, had I been willing to learn more about my father, would have whetted my curiosity but which only gave me a strange, momentary feeling of unease. I had helped serve a copious Sunday brunch for my father and his banker guest, whom he was eager to impress. It must have been at the end of World War II when news of the Jewish concentration victims was prominent in the papers. I was hanging about in the kitchen, happy not to have to sit at the table with my father and his guest (though my mother was obliged to.) I was ready to go into the dining room to clear the table when I heard what I can only describe as a howl coming from the room. I realized that my father, in reading an article aloud—my father of the stony face—had been overcome by uncontrollable sobbing. Of course, he identified with the victims. He could very well have been one of them if he hadn't fled Europe still an adolescent and he may have been thinking of those he left behind or his own elderly mother whom he perhaps sent back to Europe and who would have perished along with so many others. At my present age, free of his dominance, I can have charitable feelings for him. I regret now not knowing more about his early life. Do I even know why he brought his old mother to the United States? Was it simply to help out? If I had had more sympathy for the man, when I was told about his mother, I would have assumed that deep inside of him was that young boy who yearned to see his mother. But, then, I was incapable of regarding my father with any compassion. As we've seen, my love was focused on my mother and her suffering. Yet, what did I know of his painful experiences that made him into the adult who was my father? And, because I and my siblings only knew the tough side of his nature that was forged by circumstances of which we were totally ignorant, we could never grow close to him.

But the yearning remains for a bond with a father figure. And one suffers an entire life for the lack of one. My brother, being the only male, may have suffered the most. He never measured up to what my father required of a son or perhaps it was the other way around. My father was unable to show love and respect for his growing boy and, consequently, elicited failure in his son or what he saw as failure. Thankfully, as we've seen, my brother enjoyed the love and support of one of his parents and matured, with difficulty, into what appeared to be a successful businessman and a father himself. But the yearning for a father's recognition never left him, I'm sure of that. He was seventeen and a half years older than me and out of the house when I was growing up. However, I reconnected with him as an adult and, knowing about his youth and from remarks he'd make, and because of my own experience in the same family, I felt I understood him. One remark, an astounding one, has, in fact, stayed with me. When my husband and I visited my brother during his later years—he was in his 70s—in a conversation, he said something to this effect: "Well, of course, I don't know what love is" Or perhaps it was: "I can't love. I don't know what it is." Something so poignant, revealing an inability to love that has to have been based on childhood experiences and that he, at his late age, obviously had long given up fulfilling. It is also strangely reminiscent of my mother's remark, even in the tone of self-evidence, when I told her about Sue's overnight guest. She had indeed had the love of her father. She often spoke of him with great tenderness, but she had lived years of rejection as an adult and that was uppermost in her mind. My brother, similarly, had been the object of my mother's love but it was not sufficient to overcome his father's rejection. In fact, he didn't know what fatherly love was and, consequently, couldn't emulate it, didn't know how it felt. We suspect that, as a father, his children also suffered, not from fear but from a father who hadn't learned how to connect to his children.

Some years after my father's death—my brother, at the time of my father's death, was probably in his forties—I wrote "his story" giving expression to his loss as he might have felt it as his father's life was ending. It was also a comfort to me to put into words my own distress over what I could sense were my brother's hidden feelings and that I, having the same father, shared.

My mother and brother are connected, not only as mother and only son, but as two people who shared the same fear and anxiety dealing with a strong, dominate authority in the home. Each, in his or her way, did whatever was possible to survive.

My Brother's Story

STILL afraid. A grown man, in his forties, and still afraid. He's your brother and, to you, the cues are glaring, painful ... his steeled, agreeable manner when he's talking over business with the boss, or his quick protective silences, retreats into no-comment, when he feels the old man is eager for combat. You can see how pale he is when they are together, how he aches to be called away, if only into the next room where he can sigh, yawn, scratch himself without ridicule.

You ask yourself why he ever came home after his service in the army. We had Pearl Harbor and he volunteered. The war offered an honorable escape: four years of what was, for him, peace. When it was all over, he was on the West Coast. He could have stayed. It was further away in those days: scanty plane flights, not the highway system developed later. He had friends, could have found a job — and independence. An end to fear in the pit of his stomach, to the stony face every morning. An end to harsh criticism, to scorn. He could have been a man.

But he came home. Marrying a girl from the West Coast didn't keep him there either ... She would like to have stayed, but he convinced her to go back with him. Never a word about the years of hurt and of fear. Where could he have begun? His feelings struck him as unbecoming, unmanly. He was slipping quietly back, putting himself under lock and key, and she never knew it. She would have protested for his sake, for his own well-being. Was that why he kept silent?

It was logical enough to return home, he thought. He was walking into a thriving business. After all, he was still the boss's son! If he could put up with the old feelings and stick it out, some day he would be a rich man. Surely enough reason to want to go home.

So for fifteen years, you see him masquerading as a business man. Dependable, but on his guard, he goes to the office. Every day, it's the same thing. He hears that he'll never change, that he's never done anything right in his whole life, that he never will. And, not wanting to cross his old man there, either, he becomes known in the company for his bad decisions, his mistakes that bring extra work, that keep him harried and fatigued, that supply his father with ammunition.

But over the years, people learn. Even the incompetent son matures. He gradually makes a place for himself in the business. A winning manner, a mind that, when relaxed and secure, functions well, basic honesty — these characteristics are appreciated by business associates and develop useful contacts for his company. Does the father see any of this? No, his eyes follow old habits. He looks at his son and is disappointed. Not a fighter, never was … Doesn't know what he wants, or how to get it. He'll never be a "mensch" like the other one — the son-in-law: big, manly, with a temper ingrained from his tough years growing up in a poor section of Cleveland. An ambitious fellow: went to school nights, became an engineer. If you push that one around, watch out for the storm. Smart too. Couldn't get along without him.

For fifteen years my brother works alongside his father and his brother-in-law. He grows older, has children, lives with his fear. He almost fails to notice it anymore except by a twinge, an inner compression that he assumes will always be part of him.

Hovering about this dark center, deep inside of him, is another feeling—unmentionable—a dream too tempting to contemplate yet too delicious to shrug off: the hope that one day, when he goes into work, no one will be sitting at this father's desk, that he will no longer hear his father's voice barking out a complaint or grumbling from another office, that his car will be blissfully absent from its parking spot, that, once and for all, he will have stopped encumbering his son's life.

And then it happens. The father, all his life, strong, as they say, like an ox, doesn't feel well. He's getting old and, just like any ordinary human being, his body needs some attention. He won't see a doctor. Not him. After months of discomfort, of growing weakness, he's so sick that he can hardly get up in the morning. Only then does he finally give in ... Too late. He has cancer, an advanced case, and in a few more months is in the hospital dying.

The son takes his place. No problem. He has learned the business without his father ever having noticed. He comes to work early now. Assumes his new responsibilities with energy, with almost youthful exuberance. The brother-in-law continues to handle the technical decisions. Everything goes smoothly, but with a difference. No face cut in stone to greet and, then, to retreat from quickly. No more clenches in his stomach. His head is light. Freedom has come unexpectedly, without his making a move, an act from above. And, oh my, he's happy. He can work, can breathe, deeply, and not listen for a voice, a cough, a certain footstep. He congratulates himself on his new life.

The weeks go by. The father's brain is stopping its work, but the heart beats on, tenaciously, keeping the body alive. The son looks at this helpless, dying man and remembers the awkwardness he felt just a few months ago in his presence. Now, the father is just an old man, too weak to hold on to life for more than a few more days. Health, strength, capability have passed to the son. He is living a dream; a fairy tale ending. After long combat, he is enjoying victory that was, he suddenly feels, not so difficult to attain.

But the father's death comes slowly. The son has time to watch and to think. No longer fearful, he becomes prey to other feelings, to the stress of pity, to the unfamiliar pain of a son who sees his father dying, to a new hope that, in this critical moment, he will have some importance for his father.

The son visits the hospital often to sit, silent, by the bedside. His father, busy with death, is only dimly aware of this man who, every day, comes into his room.

The other members of the family visit with each other in the hallway. Even the favorite son-in-law avoids the body, with the rest of them. There are bitter memories in everyone's heart. The family clusters together, waiting.

The son looks at his father's face, chiseled and pale, more harsh, more angular than ever—a death mask now. On a narrow bed he sees the body with skinny limbs and swollen feet and a heart, which beats on, stubborn, refusing death. Yet today, tomorrow, the heart must rest. The body will be put away. His father will be dead. This is how it is to end. Nothing proven. Nothing said. The son came home. He worked hard, but did his father ever look at him and see a son? He comes every day and waits for his father to acknowledge him. My dearest boy … faithful child. I have wronged you. Forgive me in my last hour. I do, father, I do. Go in peace. I am here.

Suddenly the son, alert, leans forward. The dying father is mumbling, then hoarsely shouting. The son strains to understand. He is a witness but, as always, with his father, ineffectual. These last words will never be repeated, never remembered. Before death the father returns to the language of his childhood. The beginning and the end of a life meet. A closed circle, shutting out a son.

He tries to catch a few words, nevertheless. He tugs at

his memory, desperately. Listens for a phrase that is familiar, something he has learned when he heard his father speaking to old friends, or, when, as a child, his grandmother lived with them and spoke the only language she knew. If only he can recognize a phrase or two.

Ah, that he understands. "Nothing can help." That, at least, he can take away with him. But it is a meager harvest. The only son reaches out to his father, but his father turns to the wall and speaks a secret language.

The shouting stops. Silence. The son hovers over the bed, listens for breathing and, tucking this last bitter moment deep inside of him, turns to leave the room.

The funeral is a big affair. His father was an important man and, for many, a generous man as well. He gave thousands to charities, for scholarships. People come by the hundreds to share the family's undoubted sorrow. An endless line of cars follows the hearse to the cemetery. The family stands in the center of a mass of silent, listening people as the rabbi says a few words and the father's body is put into the ground.

Afterwards, the son stands in the warm spring sunshine. People press about him. He smiles broadly, greets friends, shakes hands that reach out to him. One person, then another, expresses great regard for his father. The son becomes the gracious host of an impressive garden party who realizes that his guest of honor is highly respected and even loved.

All these people who have come to see his father put to rest, what man do they hold in their minds? How could his father have deceived so many? Or was his own vision clouded by fear and bitterness. The son's surprise becomes tinged with pride. The father has died leaving the son the center of much attention. He is, after all, the only son and, for the first time, he is proud of it.

In the months that follow, his father's office changes. The

gray walls and sparse furniture disappear. The entire company building is repainted and redecorated with modern chairs and desks and wall-to-wall carpeting. The son is an efficient, successful business man. He wishes his father could see how he has widened contacts and created new business opportunities for the expanded company. He's a pretty important fellow now, as a matter of fact, but his father will never know it.

The new president of the company is, furthermore, at complete ease in the office. His employees and colleagues respect him and respond with good will to his direction. No one becomes too upset when he is impatient, loses his temper at someone's mistake or negligence. He, however, is rather surprised and almost pleased with his own anger.

"Perhaps I have a bit of the old man in me after all," he likes to say to himself.

The son sits in his father's office. In the top drawer of his large executive's desk is a dried up pen, fat and bulky, weathered-brick in color, an old-fashioned pen much used, dependable. A name is printed on the pen in clear, decisive letters: his father's name.

When you come to see him, he will surely find a reason to look into his top drawer. The pen. Startled, you recognize it. "I know that pen!" The son will lift it out of the drawer and cradle it in his hand. "… the only thing of his I have," he will say.

My father's pen holds a story for both my brother and me, a story unknown, lost. I have come to realize, at the end of this search into my mother's life and the significant family members who were part of it, that my father remains the most unknown of all. I, like my brother, were left to wonder what his last words meant. And, years before his death, when he might have shared with me the memories that were causing his heartfelt sobbing, I could have learned something about him—had I been ready, been able, to listen.

Being able to listen. Being aware. Before I end, I can't refrain from including a memory that has emerged from these thoughts. It is from my mother's last years. During my visits, we'd be chatting, she often in bed, I sitting beside her. One day, she said: "I think I'm getting smarter" as we discussed certain individuals and events. She was alert to their intent, and obviously felt her mind clicking along in a lively manner as she recognized scenarios. She felt smart and was smart, had learned from her long years of experience and, though physically disabled by her stroke, had discovered something new in herself.

Her observation has made me look at myself in what I must say is my old age. I realize that—judging from my ability to look at my father with some compassion—that I've achieved a kind of "smartness," an awareness of which I was incapable as a younger person. From the perspective of many years gone by, one can look back as if from the "outside," no longer caught up in the emotions of the living present, but able, tempered by years of experience, of simple distance from the past, to "listen" and understand. It's a consolation, along with inevitable declines, either physical or mental, with advanced years, that what they call wisdom can indeed be part of getting old. Not that I would be so presumptuous as to call myself "wise" but, like my mother, maybe a little smarter.

Though the title of this book is, "My Mother's Story," in reality it is my story. She undoubtedly would have told the tale in her own way, which would necessarily have differed. However, if she were here to read my narrative, I hope she would feel that I have been attentive and that, like her, I've learned and can look back on my own life with new understanding.

Photographs

A house similar to my mother's childhood home in Minsk. In the 1920s, Uncle Harold went back in search of their original house but it had disappeared.

My Grandfather.

My Grandfather and Grandmother. Someone wrote: "Sigmond and Mary Cohn" on top. It's the only photo I have of my mother's mother. She looks rather wan. I'm wondering if she was already ill when it was taken.

Uncle Maurice and the young woman he hoped to marry.

Uncle Harold and his beloved Marie.

Uncle Bob as a World War I pilot.

My father and mother with the first two children, Raymond and Marion, in front of a house borrowed from Aunt Fanny's second husband for a "vacation." The crease through my mother's face is, for me, a visual metaphor of her life with my father.

A family portrait. My mother and my two older sisters, Helen, around 11 years old, and Marion, perhaps 18 or so, are pleasantly disposed for the photo. My brother's sad face and mine, that of a 3- or 4-year-old, add a somber tone to the scene.

A happy moment with my big cousin, Richard, outside of my Aunt Ida's apartment house in Los Angeles.

My brother Raymond as a Second Lieutenant in World War II.

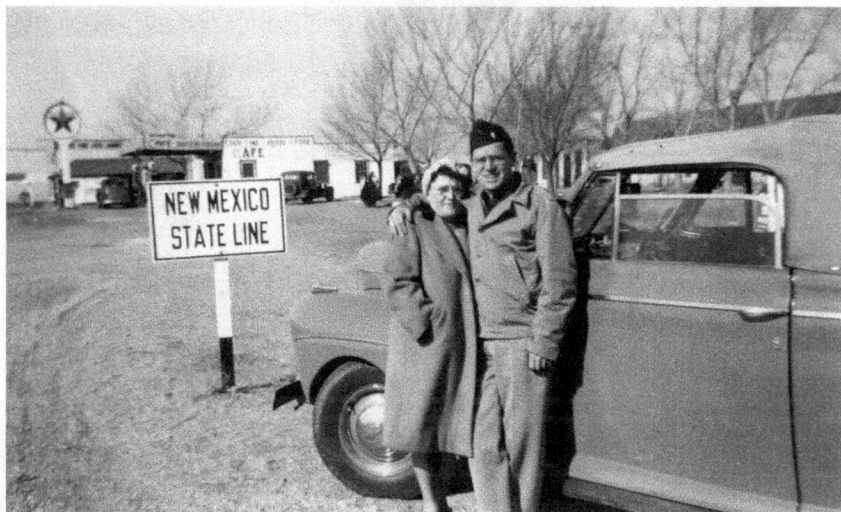

My brother and my mother on their way to California.

My Uncle Harold as a medical officer in World War II.

Uncle Al as a young, debonair fellow, perhaps at the age when his father wrote him the letter to comfort him.

Uncle Al, older, during one of his visits to us after we'd moved to the mansion, in the background. My mother, on one side, shows the affection she had for her young brother and, on the other side, is Aunt Fanny.

My mother in her 60s.

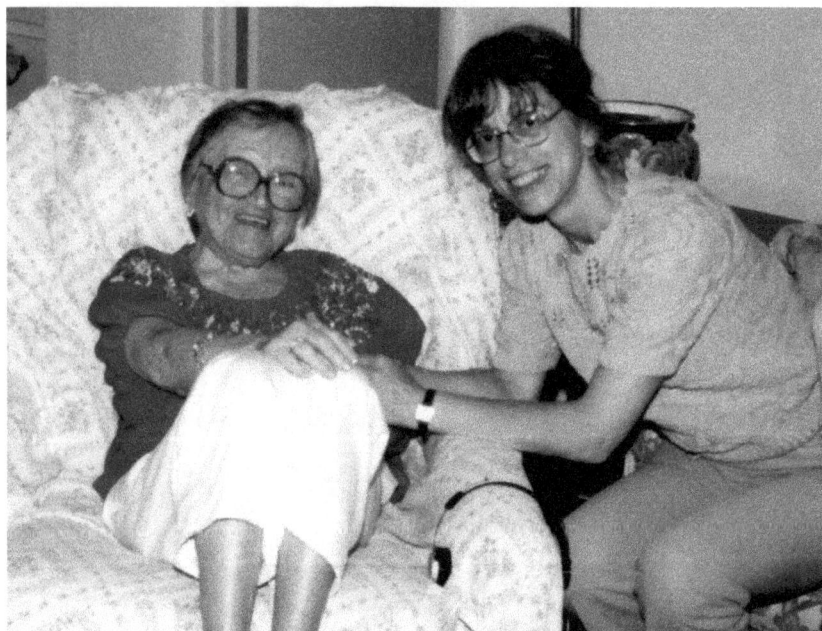

My mother, 95 or 96, with me.
It's one of the last photos I have of her.

www.ingramcontent.com/pod-product-compliance
Lightning Source LLC
Chambersburg PA
CBHW022201080426
42734CB00006B/531